© 2024 by R. A. Gilmore

ISBN: 979-8-9872766-3-1

The Cross

Verses of Awe and Wonder

R. A. Gilmore

Table of Contents

Preface

God has done some amazing things in the past, and still is doing amazing things these days. He is my inspiration and my encourager for the writing of the poems. With God leading the process, I see wonderful results from years ago that even today stir my heart as I read them.

Though I put the pen to the paper, the pen is guided by the Holy Spirit working through me. I bear the responsibility for the written words and accept the burden of any and all errors. All the honor and glory is to go to God.

For this collection of poems, I trust you find them enjoyable and perhaps some will even challenge your thinking.

God is the poet,
I am the recording secretary.

R. A. Gilmore

Foreword

One of my favorite images on Sunday mornings at the church where I serve as Lead Pastor is that of Richard Gilmore, sitting quietly in his Sunday School room, listening to God. He arrives early, even before I get there, and waits not only for his class to begin, but for God to speak to him with the poems that he pens. I look forward to reading those poems each week and noting that they were written during these quiet moments of solitude.

What a lost art in our noisy and busy societies. I'm pretty sure that Richard learned this discipline as he explored God's Word, and as he modeled his life after that of our Lord. Jesus withdrew from the business of healing, teaching, and modeling godliness, and turned to the quiet places for relationship with His Heavenly Father.

I see that intimacy in Richard's life, and in his writing. He knows what he believes and he knows the Person that he writes about. He is a quiet man that speaks loudly with his life and his writing. I am inspired by him, and I believe you will be as well.

Rev. Tommy Dove
Lead Pastor
The Grace Place Church

Introduction

The cross is the symbol of Christianity. It is also a symbol of what Christ did on the cross of Calvary – redeeming mankind by giving Himself as the Paschal Lamb to satisfy God's wrath for sinful man.

The word cross is found in both the Old Testament and the New Testament of the Bible. In the Old Testament the Aramaic word *tzlav* is found 121 times and each of these times the verb form of cross is what is proffered. In the New Testament, the Greek word is *stauros* and it is used 41 times, 9 of which are verbs and 32 are nouns. It is the noun version that is of interest for this book. That word can be found in 12 of the 27 books of the New Testament.

The first appearance in each of the four gospels is:

> Matthew 10:38
> Mark 8:34
> Luke 9:23
> John 19:17.

The next question is what was the form of the cross on which Christ was crucified? The Bible does not state the form of the cross. Several commentators have ventured into this fray using selected scriptures to defend their position.

It most likely was one of three forms known in the times of Christ. The Greek word *stauros* literally means a stake or a straight rod. Apparently the Romans were not too particular about the form of the device for execution.

There are three versions of the cross that were extant during the Roman times. One was in the shape of the Greek letter Chi and represented by the English letter X. One was in the shape of the Greek letter Tau and represented by the English letter T. The third was in the shape of the English letter t. The first of these three was later designated as St. Andrew's cross, the second as the Tau cross and the third as a Latin cross. The difference between the Tau cross and Latin cross is the placement of the transverse arm.

While the Bible does not specify the form of the cross on which Christ was crucified, many commentators claim it was the Latin cross and they base this on the fact of the placard that Pilate placed on Jesus' cross as mentioned in each of the four Gospels (Matthew 27:37; Mark 15:26; Luke 23:38; John 19:19). The form of the cross was settled by the early historians and the early artists as they used the Latin cross in their discussions and depictions.

Constantine saw a cross in his vision and that was what convinced him to become a Christian. That cross was purportedly a Latin cross. Today there are many forms of the Latin cross. Different religious groups have their specific form of the cross to proclaim their Christian identity.

The cross is not a talisman, but a reminder of Jesus' sacrificial death for our redemption. If we honor and venerate the cross, we are not following the Scripture where Christ said "take up your cross and follow Me" (Matthew 16:24; Mark 8:34; Luke 9:23). We should remember the sacrificial death and that we are to die to self to live for Christ.

It is my desire that these poems will draw you into a deeper understanding of the meaning of the cross and give you greater appreciation for the sacrifice Christ made on our behalf.

References

Analytical Concordance to the Bible
    Robert Young, 22nd American edition
    Wm B. Eerdmans Publishing
      Company
    Grand Rapids, Michigan

Matthew Henry's Commentary on the Whole Bible, vol V
    MacDonald Publishing Company
    McLean, VA

New American Standard Exhaustive Concordance of the Bible
    Robert Thomas, general editor
    Holman, Nashville, TN 1981

The Life and Times of Jesus the Messiah
    Alfred Edersheim
    Wm B. Eerdman's Publishing
      Company
    Grand Rapids, Michigan, 1974

The Westminster Dictionary of the Bible
John Davis. Revised edition by Henry
Gehman
The Westminster Press
Philadelphia, PA 1944

*Vines Expository Dictionary of Old and New
Testament Words*
W. E. Vines
Fleming Revell Company
Old Tappan, New Jersey 1981

The Cross

Stark and straight before me stood
That precious symbol made of wood.
Reminding all of years ago
The cruel fate it did bestow.
As a pin, it may be worn
Or in a necklace to adorn.
Sometimes in brass it sits up there
As a reminder for all who care.
Carried in pockets, it is indeed,
To share with one who is in need.
Could it but speak to tell its story
About its special part in glory.
It is a comfort for all who claim
And lean upon that special name.
Before it, we count all as loss,
In looking upon Calvary's cross.

The Cross

Look over there on yonder hill,
Three crosses stand so cold and still
Silhouetted against the sky,
That is where they send men to die.

I wonder what tales could be told
By those crosses so stark and bold.
Would our spirits begin to tweak
If those rough-hewn logs could but speak?

One cross carried a hardened thief
Who railed and cried in pain and grief,
Cursing the fact that he was there.
For him now life was in despair.

Then the thief on the other side
Turned to the center cross and cried,
"Oh God, forgive me please, I plead,
Because I am guilty indeed."

The center cross then shed a tear,
For the one he bore was so dear
And guilty of sin, He was not,
But He hung there our sins to blot.

From center cross, a cry aloud
Asking forgiveness for the crowd.
"Father, it is finished," He said,
And then He was mortally dead.

The King of Kings, whom the cross bore,
Laid in grave, a stone o'er the door.
But death its hold could not maintain,
And the King rose to life again.

The cross still stands against the sky,
A symbol that Christ had to die.
Sacrifice – the ransom for sin –
So we eternal life could win.

The Cross

Look over there on yonder hill,
Three wooden crosses stand stark and still.
The one in the center seems taller to me;
And is that a glow around it I see?

Why does that cross attract me so?
What is about it that I should know?
The cross is used for the common thief,
But that one seems to have borne some
   grief.

Tell me your past, old scarred dried tree.
What is the secret you hold for me?
Who is the person that you did bear,
Lifting them up so high in the air?

Hear the story that cross told me
About its agony and ecstasy.
Learn the tale, as all men should,
About this rugged piece of wood.

They took a man to court, you see,
The charge against Him, blasphemy.
The trial was brief, the verdict no,
The court was ready to let Him go.

The crowd cried out in an ugly way
That He should be crucified that day.
The court went back, but found no sin,
Yet condemned Him to quell the riotous din.

The cross was laid upon His back
And pain did all His body rack.
No shout, no plea, and no remorse.
With that load, He paced His course.

They marched Him to the mountain top
And the unruly mob never did stop
Taunting and shouting along the way.
They wanted to watch Him die that day.

On that cross of wood He was lifted high
And then He turned His face to the sky.
He called to God, "Thy will be done,
I will be Your faithful Son."

A hush upon the crowd did fall
And darkness brought its blackened pall.
A single voice then yelled aloud
And broke the silence of the crowd.

The Son of God was on that tree;
He died so He could set men free.
He paid the price, the ransom Dove,
Based on unrequited love.

That cross is there for all to see –
A symbol of love for eternity.
Whether its wood or ruby or gold,
Remember the story that's to be told.

An Old Dried Log

Out in the field an old dried log, baked by
    the sun's hot ray,
Patiently waits its future fate as it has for
    many a day.
What can await an old dried log, to what can
    it aspire –
A building piece, a toy for a child, or an
    ashen bed of fire?

That old dried log will become whatever its
    finder deems;
And each who comes along the way will
    have his own set dreams.
Some will see an old dried log, others a
    work of art.
It all depends upon your ways and what is in
    your heart.

One old dried log was fashioned by the
  skillful craftsman's hand.
He gently cut and carved and smoothed as if
  by a magical wand.
He tenderly took these finished parts and
  assembled them in his way.
He formed a manger, but it became a cradle
  full of hay.

An old dried log was carefully viewed by
  the young man standing there.
He patiently thought and held that log up in
  the air.
This for me is the log that holds the piece
  deep down inside.
"I'll set it free for all to see," said the
  carpenter with great pride.

An old dried log was roughly drawn by two
  soldiers of great might.
This will do, they both complained, for it
  was the only log in sight.
This rough old log was fashioned then into
  an ugly cross,
And it was used to crucify a man considered
  dross.

An old dried log can mean so much, and
    much it could relate
About the hands that fashioned it and
    brought it to its fate.
An old dried log captures the life of one who
    is my friend –
From cradle to carpenter to the cross – the
    Savior to the end.

Shadow of the Cross

My spirit's heavy, my soul in pain
As burdens of life pound me again.
I'm weighted down with all of life's dross,
But on yonder hill there stands a cross.

I drag weary bones across the land
And at last beneath that cross I stand.
I know not why I am standing here,
But sight of that cross my heart did sear.

The cross cries out come to me for rest,
Lay all of your burdens upon my breast,
Unladen your soul, cast off the weight,
As at the foot of the cross you wait.

I drop to my knees beneath the cross
And there my life's woes and hurts I toss.
I wail in my sorrow and my grief,
Trying to give my soul some relief.

As barren cross's shadow me does hide,
Drops of blood wash o'er me like a tide.
They cleanse, they purge, and they set me
     free.
Now Christ can use me for His glory.

The Cross

High on a hill, so bleak and so bold,
Stands an old, gnarled tree, dark and cold.
It is an emblem for all to see,
Of amazing love given so free.

It flinched with the thud of the hammer's
    throb,
As nails pierced flesh, its life signs to rob.
Three times a nail went into that tree,
And then it was raised for all to see.

A stark reminder upon the hill,
Of an empty cross, barren and still.
Symbol of faith through eternity,
Of the risen Christ who died for me.

The Symbol

Over yonder in a land far away,
In a time that is far removed from this day,
In a tiny town an event occurred
That shame, the world and its impact's still
   heard.

It was played out upon a tiny hill,
And its tremor brought a cold clammy chill.
The assembled throng was frenzied and
   wild,
But the focus was calm and not beguiled.

Emblazoned on that hill, a symbol stood,
Made out of sturdy and gnarled dark wood.
Its awesome specter displayed a great part,
And now it's emblazoned upon my heart.

The Cross

As at the foot of the cross I sit,
My soul sinks deeper into the pit.
Oh Christ, raised upon the cross so high,
Please hear my aching and lonely cry.

While into great solitude I slip,
Great drops upon my head do drip.
With my upraised hand I wipe my face,
And find crimson blood in my embrace.

I turn my gaze to the cross above
And see outstretched hands so full of love.
A weary, yet loving face I see,
As Jesus Christ gazes down on me.

In deep shame I turn my face to hide
From those gentle eyes that bore inside.
Then sweet and comforting words I hear,
"You are forgiven, to Me draw near."

My soul is refreshed, cleansed, renewed –
Great warmth floods o'er me to change my
    mood.
Once again, I gaze upon the cross –
He is gone, and so is all my dross.

The Cross

A stately cross afar does stand,
Lifted up high on yonder hill,
Silhouetted against the sky.
It stands alone so calm and still.

Nearer, nearer the cross does grow
As each step moves me to that place.
It's ambiance spreads far and wide
And casts a sense of peace and grace.

The cross is rugged, roughly hewn,
Unique in beauty and adorn.
It yielded up its awesome prey
And now stands empty, so forlorn.

Its arms and upright are stained deep
With salty streaks and darkened red.
The face is scarred, severely worn
From tears and hands of those who pled.

The Cross Upon the Hill

Boldly it stands with vistas far,
In wind or rain or still.
Its arms outstretched to welcome all –
The cross upon the hill.

In morn it casts its shadow long,
Reflected in the rill.
It basks under the sun's great light –
The cross upon the hill.

At night it casts a warming glow
That chases off the chill.
Its lights do pierce the darkened night –
The cross upon the hill.

(Written while at Lake Junaluska, NC)

The Old Tree

It was a log there on the ground,
Barren forlorn, nothing to see.
Old, forgotten, not of much use;
It was once a proud tree.

It was one always neglected.
Never was it destined to be
One that would grace a palace.
It was just an old tree.

One day it was chosen for use.
Now it was going to be free
To take its place in stately charm,
Not be just an old tree.

It was rough-hewn, then cut in two,
Placed on a hill beside the sea.
It became an old rugged cross;
Majestic was that tree.

They put the Christ on that old cross
And hung Him there for all to see.
Christ gave His life for all who want
From sin to be set free.

(Written while attending a Korean Language Walk
to Emmaus held at Redwood Glen Retreat Center,
Loma Mar, CA)

In the Shadow of the Cross

Christ named that soon one would betray;
Christ did not consider him dross.
Christ offered him love through it all
While in the shadow of the cross.

Christ walked the road in agony,
All the burdens He would not toss.
It was love that kept Him going
Under the shadow of the cross.

As we each trod the bumpy road,
Everything we can count as loss.
Christ alone is our all in all,
E'en in the shadow of the cross.

The Tree

The ax man went into the woods,
Keenly seeking for the right tree.
Trees shook at the sight of the blade;
Each wondered, would it be me?

Those sharp eyes found just the right one.
The ax was raised and planted deep.
The tree shuddered with each ax blow,
And with throbbing heart, it did weep.

The ax performed its final slice,
And the massive tree tumbled down.
The branches were sheared, thrown aside,
And now it's a log with no crown.

The log was cut, two pieces remained;
Two sizes, each straight as a rod
Were lashed together as a cross.
It bore the only Son of God.

The Cross

The cross did loom in coming days,
But only Christ did see the task.
His followers were filled with joy,
And in Christ's presence they did bask.

Each day brought that cross nearer still.
Two groups of people sought their way.
The views would soon come to a clash.
Christ, the focus, took time to pray.

The clash exploded then one day
With Christ's arrest and the sentence.
The cross loomed ever closer now;
Christ faced it all with calm presence.

Christ walked up to Cavalry's hill
Bearing the burden of the cross.
He took our guilt, He took our sin
And counted it as love, not loss.

(Palm Sunday)

The Cross

Oh that cross, that old rugged tree,
Boldly it stood upon the hill.
Outstretched arms to welcome its prey,
To embrace and then, yet to kill.

The Christ was the advancing prey;
The cross shuddered and then it was ill.
The old cross had a role to play,
And it was to follow God's will.

As the Christ's life did ebb away
That old cross shed many a tear.
It had done its job, paid the price,
And the old rugged cross did disappear.

The Cross

The cross did hold Him ever tight
To be sure He would not take flight.
He hung there in great agony,
Bearing the guilt of you and me.

Beaten and alone He hung,
Calling out with dry parched tongue.
From that cross He ne'er tried to flee,
'Twas our path to eternity.

Now that cross is naked, bare,
For the Christ is no longer there.
The cross gave up its sacred prey,
And to heaven Christ paved the way.

The Cross

The cross is not the Christian faith,
It is a symbol of God's love.
It reminds us of Christ's great work
Journeying on earth from above.

Christ was crucified on the cross
Then was placed in a borrowed grave,
He conquered sin and conquered death
And rose to life mankind to save.

Why did the Christ stay on the cross?
What actually kept Him there?
'Twas not the nails that pierced His flesh,
But love for sinners ev'rywhere.

Christ took our guilt and took our shame
And took our place upon the cross.
He thus became our atonement,
Taking away all of our dross.

Christ did suffer on our behalf
To free us from the load of sin.
He gave His life, stood in our place,
For us, eternal life did win.

(Written while visiting Marilyn and Tom Dumm in
Naples FL)

The Cross

When Jesus Christ hung on that cross,
It wasn't nails that held Him there.
It was not the Sanhedrin's words,
Nor was it guards' spears ev'rywhere.

It wasn't Pilate's yielding words,
'Twas not the disciples despair,
'Twas not fear of the angry mob,
It was not due to lack of prayer.

So many thought this was the end,
But hanging there was not a loss.
He did it all for you and me.
'Twas love that held Christ on the cross.

The Tree

The tree was stately, straight and tall.
It gazed over the forest land.
It wondered just what it would be
Once felled by the lumberman's hand.

It felt the draw shave's scraping blade
As the thick bark the blade did flay.
It endured the hot searing teeth
As its size the saw cut away.

When the chisel did strike and tear
The tree did quiver and did shake.
Each hammer blow did rive the wood
As men their product they did make.

The tree looked down, began to weep,
Its aspirations were a loss.
It suffered deep indignity
For it was now a rugged cross.

It bore the body of a man
And stood there in complacency.
It was now just a tool for men
To show man's inhumanity.

The cross then overheard some words –
Its prey was not just a mere man.
It truly was the Son of God
Carrying out His Father's plan.

The cross then warmly did embrace
This Christ that hung upon its bough.
It desperately tried to help
But it really did not know how.

The Christ was taken from the cross
And placed into a nearby grave.
The cross heaved and mourned, shed great
   tears
For the one the cross tried to save.

The cross is empty on the hill.
With dignity it stands in view.
Christ's blood left a stain on the cross.
The cross's tears left a stain too.

The Cross

The cross is where the Christ did die,
Bearing the burden of our sin.
In spite of all our guilt and shame,
He died for us that life we'd win.

Christ was the perfect Paschal Lamb,
Unblemished 'till He bore our guilt.
That rugged cross is barren now;
Christ rose to life and death did wilt.

The cross, a symbol of our faith,
Where we can daily cast our dross.
There we confess our guilt and shame,
Leaving it all beneath the cross.

At the cross we can be washed clean.
At the cross our life is renewed.
At the cross Christ's love can be found,
Into our life that love's imbued.

Christ does invite us to the cross
Where we can begin life anew.
Therefore have you dealt with the cross
And has the cross now dealt with you?

The Cross

The cross was straight, stately and tall.
It did stand out in any crowd.
It rose higher than those around,
Because of this, it became proud.

It wanted to be the best cross
With all the honors it could show.
It desired to be number one,
Among the others it would glow.

It was selected for a task
And would bring honor to a king.
It would outshine competitors
And such great glory it would bring.

The cross was taken to a hill
Where it could reach up to the sky
And stretch its arms across the way
And seen by ev'ry passerby.

Criminals were marched to the hill,
Three men who were sentenced to die.
The cross was aghast, felt the shame,
Demoralized, sensed its end nigh.

Guilt shakingly ran down the arms
As the cross sensed it was abused.
From those strong arms the fame had fled
As sorrow and shame became fused.

The cross then heard a sobbing cry
That burned its heart, yet made it sing.
A flicker of hope for the cross,
The one it bore was called a king.

The struggling crowd looked at the man
The cross was not the central sight.
It was on the man the cross bore
The cross had lost all of its might.

The crowd still milled about the place
Thus many feet near the cross trod.
The cross felt strong and glad of heart
He was bearing the Son of God.

(Written while visiting Marilyn and Tom Dumm
in Mayville, NY)

Crosses

Look over there on yonder hill
Three crosses stand so stark and still.
When convicted, after they're tried,
Culprits come here, hung 'till they've died.

Three were brought to this lonely place
And they were hung with much disgrace.
Two cried in pain as nails were pound,
The other uttered not a sound.

Two ranted about being there,
The third offered a solemn prayer.
Two were deserving of their plight,
The third was there because of spite.

Of the two, one knew he would pay
For his errors along life's way.
He pleaded relief for his vice,
One said they'd join in paradise.

Three men each hanging on a cross,
They were just society's dross.
Each one did die while hanging there,
Death of the one brought much despair.

The third day early in the morn
The one death's shackles He had shorn.
Bright light stepped from the darkened cave
And all mankind the Christ did save.

(Written while sitting in the sanctuary of
Covenant Presbyterian Church, Nashville, TN)

The Cross

The cross is a sign and symbol
Of what God did to set us free.
Our sins were nailed upon that cross
For redemption for you and me.

Upon that cross the Christ did die
And then was placed into the grave.
The cross and grave could not contain
For Christ did rise, mankind to save.

See the cross, remember the Christ
And His salvation for our sin.
Remember that He died for us,
For us eternal life did win.

(Written at Covenant Presbyterian Church,
Nashville, TN)

The Cross

Ah, the cross, that heinous wood cross,
Where our Lord Christ was crucified.
A symbol of the price Christ paid
So God's wrath would be satisfied.

Oh that cross, it hangs empty now.
A symbol of God's gracious love,
Shows that we've been bought for a price
By Christ who now reigns up above.

Oh the cross, that strong sacred cross,
Reminds us that each step we trod
We have a Savior strong and true,
A Savior who's the Son of God.

(Written at Covenant Presbyterian church,
Nashville, TN)

The Cross

Oh that cross, that old rugged cross,
Stained, smudged over many a year.
Bedraggled and forlorn it stands
Yet it's a symbol we hold dear.

In many forms that cross appears
Presenting in many a size.
It's admired, sometimes it's adorned,
Even now brings tears to the eyes.

Oh that cross, that stately sweet cross,
What ere the form it does display
We grasp it firmly, hold it fast
Rememb'ring Christ our guide and stay.

(Written at Covenant Presbyterian Church,
Nashville, TN)

Symbols

The cross is the transition point,
The cave the door to victory.
These symbols God has put to use
For His great change in history.

The cross is where the Christ did die
After the trial of infamy.
From man's view 'twas a tragic loss
From God's, 'twas a necessity.

These symbols are our foundation,
Pillars on which we build our life.
The life we build can be quite sad
Or that life can be very rife.

Victory

It was just some pieces of wood,
On Calvary's hill it had stood.
More than just pieces of timber,
It was a sight to remember.

Pieces were fitted as a cross,
A stark stately symbol of loss.
Though the cross inflicted much pain,
It is still a symbol of gain.

On that cross they lifted Christ high
Making sure that there He did die.
They put Christ's body in a cave,
A borrowed tomb served as His grave.

That tomb the Christ could not contain
And the Christ rose to life again.
Christ conquered all of death and sin
And for us salvation did win.

(Written at Covenant Presbyterian Church,
Nashville, TN)

The Cross

There's the cross, emblazoned on high
Stately on the hill it does stand.
A stark symbol of misery
And a symbol of love so grand.

Upon that cross the Savior bled,
On that cross Christ was crucified.
On that cross sorrow and love joined,
On that cross the Redeemer died.

Upon that cross my sins were nailed,
There forgiveness did set me free.
Thus on that cross Christ took my place
And on that cross Christ died for me.

(Written at Tulip Grove Baptist Church,
Old Hickory, TN)

The Cross

It was large, hand hewn was the span,
It stood taller than any man.
Nothing but ill did this thing bode,
It was a very heavy load.

They hung my Lord upon that tree
And placed it there for all to see.
They pierced His side, He gave a sigh,
"It is finished" was His last cry.

The Lord was put to death right there
Leaving emptiness and despair.
The disciples were at a loss,
Their hopes had been dashed on the cross.

On this day it is plain to see
Christ's death on the cross was for me.
Christ's blood cleanses me from my sin
And eternal life I did win.

Forgiveness

The cross over on yonder hill
Is an old rugged wooden cross.
That cross, stark and empty it stands
Is a place to lay down our dross.

Like the cross on Calvary stood,
Bearing the weight of God's own Son,
The cross has become a symbol,
Not of loss but of vic'try won.

We can take our sins to the cross,
There unburden our weary soul.
Christ will forgive, lighten our load,
If our life we let Him control.

(Written at the home of Sarah and John Avery,
Brentwood, TN)

The Cross

Christ took the burden of the cross
Carried it to Calvary's hill.
Then on the cross Christ was nailed
Hung there until His breath was still.

We're called daily to take our cross[1]
And that the cross would not be void.[2]
Our cross should show the pow'r of God,[3]
The cross which Christ did not avoid.[4]

The world's been crucified to you
And you're crucified to the world.[5]
Live for Christ, and endure the shame
And the taunts that sinners have hurled.

---

1. Luke 9:23
2. 1 Corinthians 1:17
3. 1 Corinthians 1:18
4. Hebrews 12:2
5. Galatians 6:14

Symbols

Cross, a symbol of heinous death.
Cross, where Jesus drew His last breath.
Cross, a sign of Christ's sacrifice.
Cross, Christ's death for us did suffice.

Christ took our sins and sorrows too.
Christ bore our guilt, for us in lieu.
Christ bore God's wrath, God's cup to drain.
Christ died for us without disdain.

Confession is what we must do.
Confession helps us follow through.
Confession cleanses heart and soul.
Confession shows God's in control.

The Cross

Holy Father, You sent Your Son
To Your people, them to redeem.
What Christ taught, leaders rejected,
For Your will they had no esteem.

The Christ pursued living Your will
And showing how to live in love.
The leaders would not accept Christ
Nor that He came from heav'n above.

The leaders pursued their own way,
As for Christ, they spilled His blood.
They crucified Him on a cross
Now through the cross blessings flood.

(Written at Grace Place Church)

The Symbol

It's a symbol of heinous death,
That stifles life through our last breath.
Suffocation will do you in
And then relief as death does win.

It's also a symbol of life,
Of conquered sin, relief of strife.
The entry into life anew,
With bright eternity in view.

It is the way to remove dross,
It is the win, it's not a loss.
It is not just some shiny gloss,
It's the Lord Jesus Christ's own cross.

(Written at the Donelson-Hermitage YMCA)

www.ingramcontent.com/pod-product-compliance
Lightning Source LLC
LaVergne TN
LVHW051203080426
835508LV00021B/2776